Handmade
Metal & Wire
Greetings Cards

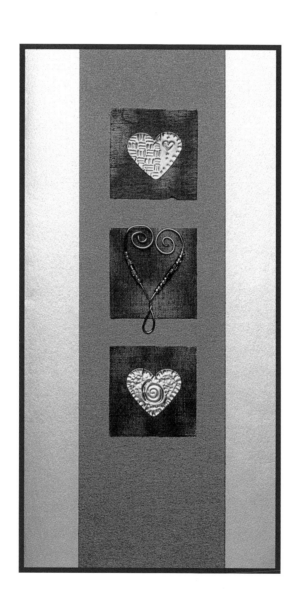

I need to thank my wonderful husband Mervyn and my boys, Matthew and Owen, for putting up with me and all the mess at home while I was writing my book.
Thank you too for all the enthusiasm and support from my good friend Melanie and all my crafting friends, too many to mention individually.
I dedicate my book to Mervyn, Matthew, Owen, Mum, Dad, Shine and to the memory of Laurie.

Enjoy!

Handmade
Metal & Wire
Greetings Cards

Julie Hickey

SEARCH PRESS

First published in Great Britain 2002

Search Press Limited
Wellwood, North Farm Road,
Tunbridge Wells, Kent TN2 3DR

Text copyright © Julie Hickey
Photographs by Lotti de la Bédoyère, Search Press Studios
Front cover and spine photographs by
Roddy Paine Photographic Studios
Photographs and design copyright © Search Press Ltd. 2002

ISBN 1 903975 01 8

If you have difficulty obtaining any of the equipment or
materials mentioned in this book, please write to the
Publishers, at the address above, for a current list of stockists,
including firms which operate a mail-order service.

Publishers' note
All the step-by-step photographs in this book feature the
author, Julie Hickey, demonstrating how to make
handmade greetings cards. No models have been used.

ACKNOWLEDGEMENTS

*With thanks to Jeremy Lowe at Royal Sovereign,
Peter Clark at Kars & Co., Judith Brewer at
Woodware Toys and Gifts and especially to
Sue Taylor at Craftwork Cards, for supplying all the
products that I needed to complete my book.
Without all your support and help I would not have
been able to fulfil my dream and write this book.*

*I also want to thank the whole team at
Search Press, but especially Sophie, Juan and Lotti
for all their patience and hard work during
photography. The time and effort put in was well
worth it for the end result. I also want to thank
Roz Dace for believing in me and giving me the
chance to write this book.*

Thank you.

Printed in Spain by A. G. Elkar S. Coop. 48180 Loiu (Bizkaia)

Contents

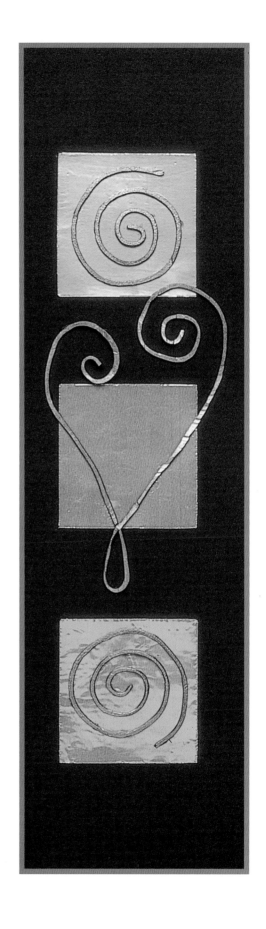

Introduction

Six years ago my then boss, Maggie Wright, took me to Dallas to attend a craft trade show. For four days before the show we stayed with her good friend, Vesta Abel, in Tucson, Arizona. During these four days, Vesta introduced me to many new stamping techniques and products. The materials that had me totally hooked were sheets of copper metal. The techniques Vesta used on them were quite simply amazing, and the results fascinated me. Techniques from quilting to embossing could be applied to the metal, and stunning things happened when you heated it. Vesta's work really was art from her heart.

Several years later and again at a craft trade show, this time in Anaheim, California, I met with Jana Ewy. She was using the copper with coloured foil sheets and adding wire accents to her outstanding work. Jana had taken the products to a new level and left me feeling totally inspired.

These two incredibly talented ladies are totally responsible for my love of metal and wire. I have taken all that I have learned from these remarkable ladies and turned it into my own creative projects. I hope you will enjoy them and that they will inspire you to see what you can achieve with metal and wire.

Materials

Metal and foil

Metal is available in copper, brass, pewter and aluminium and comes in both light and medium weights.

I love working with the copper metal, because it is pure copper, and when heated it changes from its bright copper colour to tarnished orange, then to pink, purple and blue and finally to silvery gold.

Metal can be embossed or quilted, and cut or punched in to a wide variety of shapes.

Coloured foils are much thinner and lighter weight than the metals. Various colours are available, including purple, blue, turquoise, red and green. The foils are coloured only on one side; they are silver on the reverse. The foils need to be treated with care as they mark and scratch easily. You cannot change the colour of the foils by heating them.

Mesh

Mesh comes in various colours including copper, brass and aluminium. The copper in mesh is pure and can be heated to change the colour. The size of the mesh holes varies from woven, like fabric, to 3.2mm (1/8in) and 6.3mm (1/4in) openings. Mesh can be used to shape around objects to form structures, for instance, if you have a favourite bowl and would like another the same, form the mesh around it and the mesh will hold the shape.

I use mesh as accents or backgrounds for my work.

Wire

Wire is available in many gauges and colours, and is easy to bend and shape. The higher the gauge number, the thinner the wire, e.g. 26g is thinner than 18g. Wire is sold by length and by weight, in pounds or kilos.

Found objects

I generally keep my eyes open for any objects I can use in my artwork. I love beach combing for shells, pebbles and driftwood, or picking up twigs and leaves from country walks. Foil sweet wrappers and the foil round Easter eggs are brilliant to use – and what an excuse to eat chocolate!

Card and paper

Use colours you enjoy and that work with the metal, foil and wire you have used. Card can by smooth or textured, plain or patterned. You can use vellum, parchment, handmade or mulberry papers. See Making cards on pages 12–13 for more details.

Glitter glue

This is ultra-fine glitter mixed with glue, and comes in a wide variety of colours. Shake the bottle before using it to ensure that the glue is at the nozzle end. This will stop air bubbles from spoiling your work.

Card, ready-made card blanks and luggage labels, and a selection of found objects: shells, driftwood, sweet wrappers, feathers and fossils.

Beads

The beads I have used when wrapping the wire around my work are seed beads. These are small beads that work well with 26g wire, and they come in many colours. They can be transparent or opaque in finish – just choose a colour that works with your card, metal and wire colours.

Beads, buttons and bits make wonderful accents for your cards, and glitter glue adds sparkle.

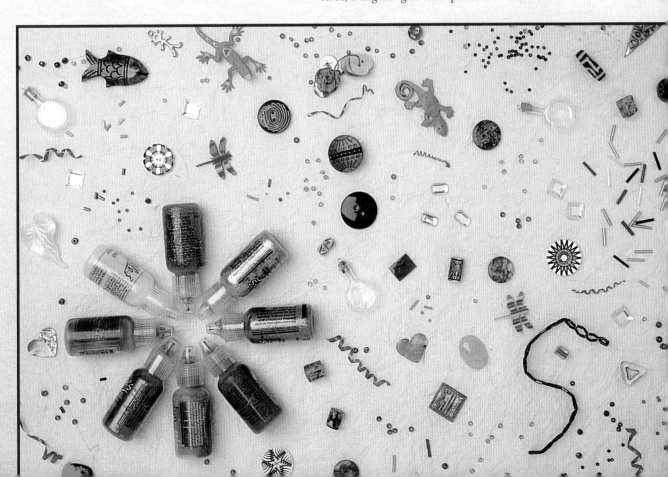

Other items

A craft **heating tool** is used to heat the copper metal or mesh, as it gives you the greatest control over the colour change. Always protect work surfaces with something heat-proof like a **chopping board**. A gas or electric hob or a hot air gun paint stripper can also be used, but these change the colour very quickly, so the metal needs to he held 10–15cm (4–6in) away from the heat.

An **embossing tool** is a wooden handle with a metal ball on either end, usually in different sizes. It is used to create patterns, quilted and hammered effects on metal and foil. A **foam sheet** must be used when using the embossing tool. The soft foam absorbs the metal or foil and gives a more pronounced effect.

A shaped **wooden tool** can be used to stretch the metal to give it more of a 3D effect.

A **crimper** is a plastic or metal roller which, when the handle is turned, gives a corrugated effect to metal, foil and 22g or 26g wire.

A **brayer** can be used to remove creases and folds from metal or foil.

A **piercing tool** has a sharp metal point on a wooden handle, and is used to create holes in metal and foil for a punched, pierced effect.

A **craft knife** is used for cutting cards, metal, foil and mesh. A **self-healing cutting mat** should be used. It's a hard, firm surface, which when cut into, heals the cut marks.

Plain or **soft-grip scissors** are used to cut the metal and foil. **Decorative scissors** add interest to your artwork and can be used on card, metal foil or mesh.

Punches are metal cutters that can be used with card, metal, foil and mesh to give you different shapes, such as daisies, squares, hearts, spirals, leaves and many more.

3D fluid is used when creating a rubbing. It helps to support your metal and fill in the back of the shape to stop it from denting.

Round-nosed pliers are used to bend and shape wire. If you get unwanted kinks in your wire, simply pull it through the plastic jaws of some **straightening pliers**. **Wire cutters** are best for cutting wire, since if you use scissors, you will damage them.

A **modeller's hammer** and **anvil** are used to flatten wire and give it a beaten look.

A **bone folder** is a shaped piece of bone that is used to score (in the upright position) and fold (used on its side) cards.

Pencils are used to mark card when folding and scoring and also for tracing patterns from this book, using **tracing paper**. A **plastic eraser** is used to remove pencil marks from cards, but do not use it on metallic cards, as it will mark them. A **metal ruler** is used when cutting cards, metal, foil and mesh to ensure they are straight. It can also be used for tracing straight lines in patterns. A **set square** is used for mounting artwork on to cards.

All-purpose craft glue is used to stick embellishments to cards, including wire accents. A **glue pen** can be used when precision is needed to apply small pieces of paper and card.

Double-sided tape is used to adhere card, paper, metal, foil and mesh to cards. **Spray mount** is an aerosol glue, which I use when attaching thin and fine paper, mulberry papers, sweet papers and any handmade papers. You apply a fine, even layer of glue to the reverse side of your work and it lies flat on your card. It is also excellent for adhering vellum or parchment papers to cards, as you cannot see the glue. **3-D foam tape** is used to stick metal, foil and mesh, or card and papers to your work. It gives added dimension as it does not lie flat on your card.

A **guillotine** is used to cut card and paper to the correct size. A **paper trimmer** is a type of small guillotine. It can also be used for scoring card if you remove the blade and replace it with a bone folder or scoring blade.

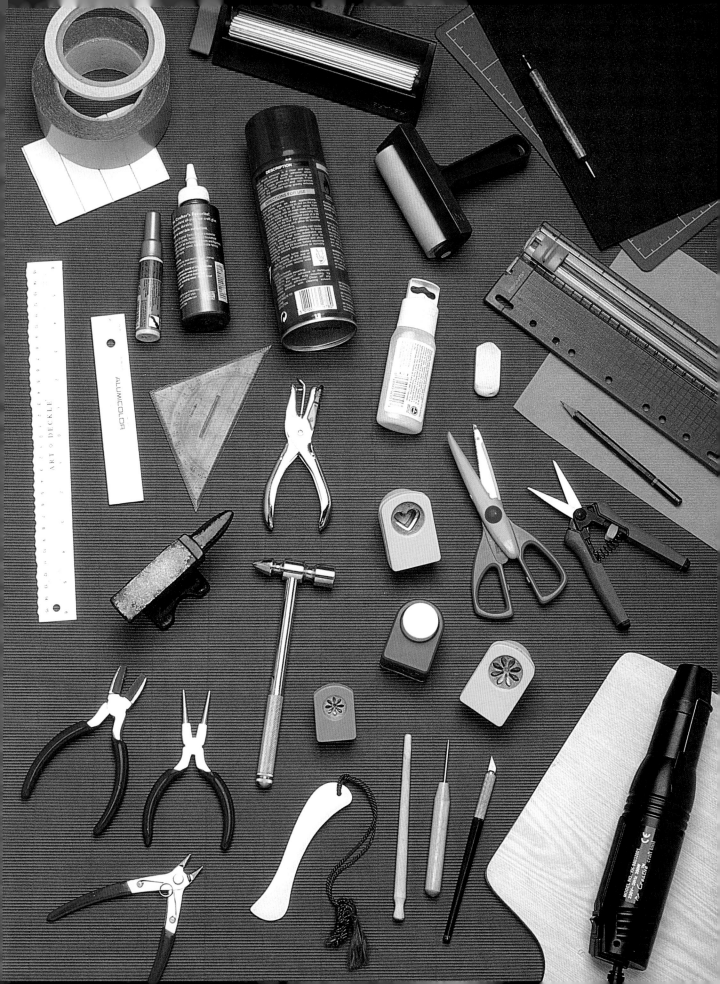

Making cards

The card on to which you mount your artwork is as important as the artwork itself. Many people try to cut corners and use cheap card – don't! If you have spent your precious creative time making a piece of artwork, it deserves to be mounted on the best quality card you can afford.

There are so many colours and textures of card available now, you really are spoilt for choice. Choose a colour that works well with your artwork. This can make or break the finished look of your card.

The card has to be of a weight that can support your artwork. The copper metal can make it quite heavy, so a thin card would buckle and bend. The weights of card vary from colour to colour and between different textures too. This means that there is no magic number to work from, but around 160gsm is a good average weight card, and dark coloured card will probably need to be more like 240gsm.

Once you have chosen a card in the colour you want, of a weight to support your artwork, test it to feel how firm it is, making sure that it will not bend too much.

You will need
Card
Paper trimmer
or craft knife, metal ruler and cutting mat
Pencil
Plastic eraser
Bone folder
Double-sided tape
Set square

Scoring and folding

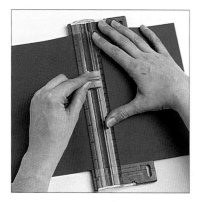

1. Cut your card to size using a paper trimmer, or a metal ruler and a craft knife, on a self-healing cutting mat.

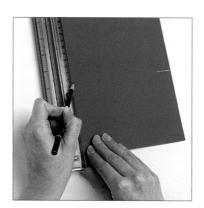

2. Measure your card to find the centre, and put a small pencil mark at the top and bottom.

3. Remove the blade from the paper trimmer and place the card under the trimmer guide. Place a bone folder in an upright position in the cutting groove and pull it down to the bottom of the card several times. Apply only light pressure.

4. Remove the card and you will see a groove called 'the valley'. This is the front of your card. Rub off the pencil marks with a plastic eraser.

5. Turn the card over and you will see a bulbous line. This is 'the mountain,' and this is always on the inside of the card. Put the edges of the card together and use the bone folder on its side to flatten the fold of the card. This will give it a sharp, crisp edge.

Mounting

1. To mount card to card, apply double-sided tape to all the edges of the card to be mounted. Pull the paper backing off just a little. Working from the front, you can see little tabs showing.

2. Place this card on your folded card. Since only parts of the double-sided tape are exposed, you can move it around to position it. When you are happy with the position, firm the exposed corners down. Hold the card in place and gently pull the tabs of backing paper away. Now firm along all the edges.

3. Use a set square to mark the position of your finished artwork. This set square has ruler markings that work from the nought in the centre outwards in both directions. This makes it easy to place your artwork in the centre of your card.

Metal techniques

Rubbing

Found objects can be great to create rubbings from. It is easier with foil than with metal sheets. Place the foil over your found object, such as a shell, and use the wooden tool or embossing tool to rub and trace the patterns and markings on it.

Heating

You can only do this with pure copper. Using a craft heating tool, electric or gas hob or hot air gun paint stripper, heat the metal. It will change from bright copper to burnished orange to pink and then to purple. Finally it goes from blue to silvery gold.

Hammering

Create wonderful texture on the metal or foil by hammering. Use the large end of the embossing tool while resting on the foam sheet, and hammer the metal. Work so that the markings are close together.

Punching

Use different shaped metal cutters to cut out shapes in metal and foil.

Embossing

Use the embossing tool to create patterns on the metal or foil with a foam sheet beneath your work to help absorb the pattern.

Crimping

Feed the metal or foil through the rollers of the crimper to create a fabulous corrugated effect.

Wire techniques

Crimping
Feed the wire through the rollers on the crimper, and hey presto! Beautifully crimped wire. This works best with 22g or 26g wire.

Hammering
Once you have bent and shaped some wire, you can use a hammer and anvil to give your work a beaten look. This works best with 18g and 22g wire.

Winding and wrapping
I have used 26g wire to wrap around metal and foil. I found it easier to attach the end of the wire to the back of the piece with double-sided tape before beginning.

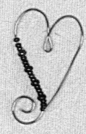

Beading
I used seed beads when wrapping my work, so I needed 26g wire. If you use bigger beads, you could change to 22g wire.

Sparkle
Add glitter glue to a piece of shaped and beaten wire to give extra sparkle and lift to your work.

Bending and shaping
Round-nosed pliers are great to start the bending and shaping of the wire, then let your fingers take over. This works well with 18g, 22g and 26g wire.

Burnished Daisy

This daisy card is an easy project to get you started. Using just a few techniques, you will start your creative journey into metal and wire cards. You will learn to cut, trace, emboss and heat the copper metal to create this stunning card. Having made this daisy card, you will be filled with confidence to continue with the more involved projects.

You will need

Copper metal (1 sheet)

Card: A4 size black, fuchsia and purple

Scissors

Pencil • Plastic eraser

Tracing paper

Embossing tool • Foam sheet

Heating tool • Chopping board

Double-sided tape

Craft knife • Cutting mat

Metal ruler

Paper trimmer

Heating tool safety

Always heat metal on a heat-proof surface such as a chopping board. Remember that the metal conducts the heat, so if you are holding it with your fingers, keep them well away from the area you are heating. You can hold the metal with a wooden peg to be absolutely safe.

The pattern for the Burnished Daisy card

16

1. Cut the copper to size with a craft knife and metal ruler, on a cutting mat. You can also use scissors. The design is 10.5cm² (4¹/₈in²), but leave some space around the edges.

2. Trace the pattern. Lay the tracing on the copper and place the copper on a foam sheet. Emboss the pattern using the medium point of an embossing tool.

3. Put the embossed copper on to a heat-proof surface such as a chopping board. Heat the copper with a heating tool and watch as the colours change.

4. Heat the copper all over until it turns a burnished orange colour. As soon as the area you are heating turns this colour, move on to the next part.

5. Next, direct the heat on to specific areas to change the colour further. After the orange, the copper turns pink.

6. Heat the squares in the corners of the design until they turn silver.

Using the heating tool

Hold the heating tool 2.5cm (1in) away from the copper sheet when heating it.

8. Apply double-sided tape to the back of the copper. Cut a 11cm^2 (4^3/$_8$in^2) piece of fuchsia card. Peel back the ends of the backing paper from the double-sided tape, and place the copper on the fuchsia card (see Mounting on page 13).

7. Cut round the design using a craft knife and metal ruler on a cutting mat. Be careful as the edges of the copper can be very sharp.

9. Cut a 12cm^2 (4^3/$_4$in^2) piece of purple card and mount the fuchsia card on it in the same way.

10. Mount the purple square on your black card, which should be cut to 26 x 13cm, (10^1/$_4$ x 5in) and scored and folded to make a 13cm square.

Opposite
A simple design like this, which is easy to trace, can be transformed into a stunning card, simply by heating the pure copper sheet.

Two of these cards were made using only part of the daisy pattern: one features the central flower, another uses two borders placed together. The card on the far right has a similar border, but shows different patterns created using the embossing tool. Don't forget to decorate your envelopes to match.

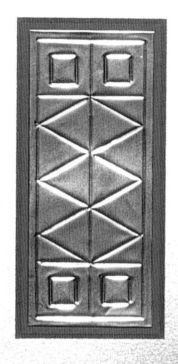

Jewelled Butterfly

This jewel-bright butterfly involves tracing, cutting and embossing as before. Hammering metal, bending and shaping wire and adding glitter glue are the new techniques in this project.

When you have made the butterfly, you could try designing your own bug – a dragonfly or bumble bee would look fantastic.

The patterns for the jewelled butterfly and its antennae

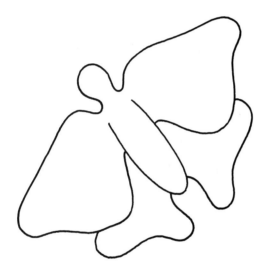

You will need

Copper metal, 1 sheet

Square copper card blank
12cm² (4¾in²)

Card: A4 turquoise

Copper wire, 22g, 20.3cm
(8in) long

Glitter glue: turquoise, purple,
magenta and copper

Soft-grip scissors

Pencil • Plastic eraser

Tracing paper

Embossing tool • Foam sheet

Double-sided tape

3D foam tape

Round-nosed pliers

Wire cutters

Paper trimmer

Tip
You could heat the butterfly, as it is made with pure copper and will change colour for you as in the Burnished Daisy project.

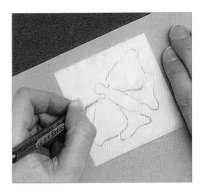

1. Trace the pattern and transfer it on to the metal using the medium point of an embossing tool on a foam sheet.

2. Cut the metal butterfly shape out using soft-grip scissors.

3. Mark the wings of the butterfly using the embossing tool as shown.

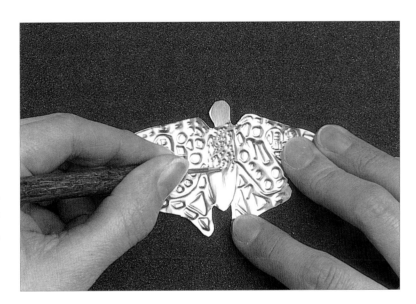

4. Hammer the body using the embossing tool. Resting on the foam sheet, stab the metal with the larger end of the tool to create the hammered effect.

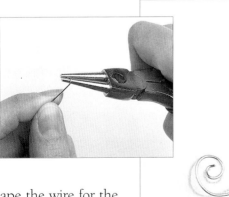

5. Bend and shape the wire for the butterfly's antennae, using the pattern as a guide. Start the curl at the end of the wire with the round-nosed pliers, then use your fingers to complete the shape.

7. Place a piece of 3D foam tape on the reverse of the butterfly's body.

6. Stick the antennae to the reverse of the butterfly's head with a piece of 3D foam tape.

8. Apply glitter glue to the butterfly in different colours and leave it to dry for approximately twenty minutes.

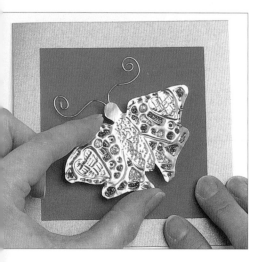

9. Cut a square of turquoise card 9cm^2 (3½in^2) and mount it on to your copper card using double-sided tape. Peel off the backing from the 3D foam tape and mount the butterfly on the turquoise square. Bend the wings slightly so that your work looks more dimensional and does not lie flat on the card.

Having acquired the skills of embossing and hammering metal, and bending and shaping wire, you can create your own bug cards. The subtle use of glitter glue can add a natural-looking sparkle.

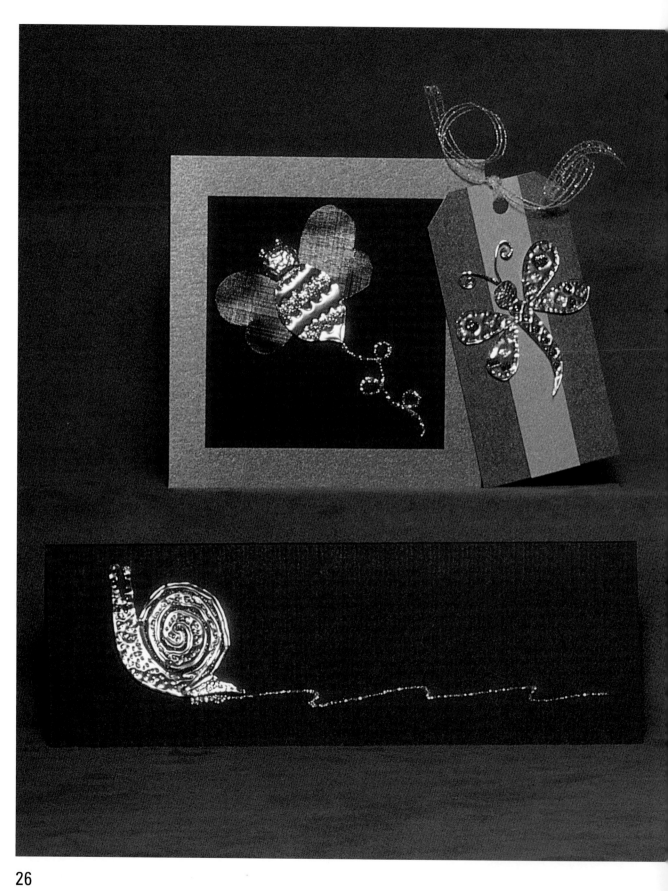

Go wild with bugs! The bee card combines natural copper with gold glitter glue to create shimmering stripes, and heated copper mesh makes beautiful wings. The glitter glue snail's trail adds a touch of fun, and really stands out against the black card. Jewel-bright colours against silver make a vibrant dragonfly card.

Beaded Squares

I love the way that, each time you heat the copper metal, you get different results.

By heating a sheet of copper and then punching out squares, you will have many variations of random colour on your card.

New techniques in this project include crimping wire, wrapping with wire and adding beads to give another dimension to your work.

Tip
Try wrapping different shapes with wire. Leaves work really well. See the Oak Leaf card on page 32.

See the Oak Leaf card on page 32.

You will need

Copper metal (1 sheet)

Black square card blank: 13cm^2 (5^1/$_8$in^2)

Cardboard 2.5cm (1in) squares

Red 26g wire (1 reel)

Seed and bugle beads

Scissors

Heating tool • Chopping board

Metal ruler

Craft knife

Square punch

Crimper

Double-sided tape

Wire cutters

1. Heat a piece of copper, applying more heat in some areas than others, in order to achieve a variety of colour effects, from burnished orange to purple to silvery blue.

2. Punch nine squares using a square hole punch.

3. Apply double-sided tape to the cardboard tiles. Peel off the backing and stick the tiles to the copper squares.

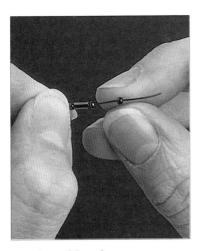

4. Thread beads on to a piece of uncrimped wire.

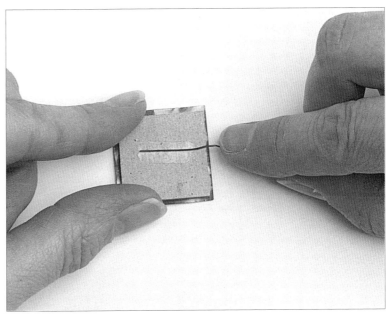

5. Put a piece of double-sided tape on the back of one of the copper-covered tiles and stick the end of the beaded wire to it.

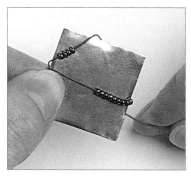

6. Wrap the beaded wire round the square so that the beads show at the front. Trim with wire cutters and secure at the back with another piece of double-sided tape.

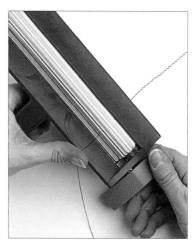

7. Crimp a piece of the red wire using a crimper.

8. Wrap some of the copper tiles with beaded wire, some with crimped wire and some with plain wire. Leave some of them unwrapped. Mount the squares on your card using double-sided tape.

The variation in the colours of the metal, set off by plain, crimped and beaded wire, creates this stunning card.

Put your new skills to work and create very different-looking cards, using the same techniques. Shaped, beaded wire creates beautiful plant forms in the butterfly card, whilst punched card sets off the heated copper square. Wrapped, heated copper hearts make a lovely card for Valentine's Day, a wedding or anniversary. Nine copper squares are stuck directly on to a shimmering gun-metal grey card, and set off with a beaded wire heart accent. Leaf shapes are great for wrapping with wire: this one is also mounted on open 6.3mm (¼in) mesh.

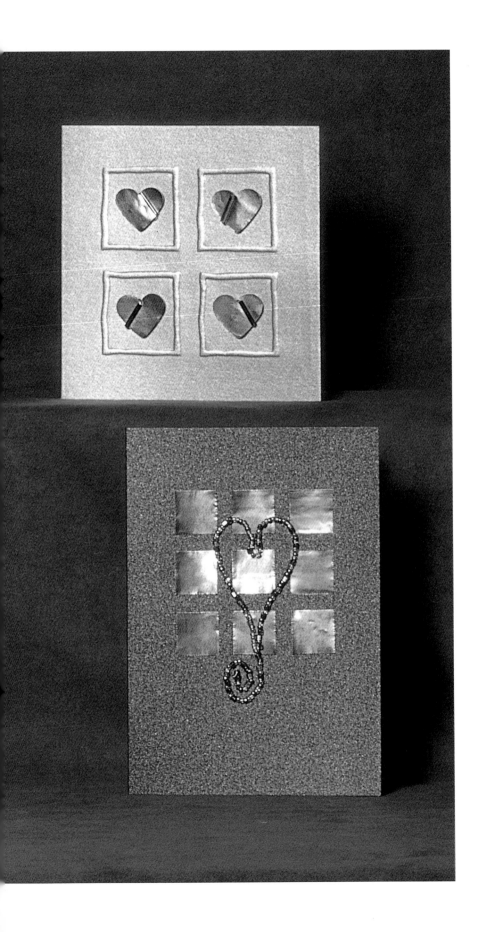

Purple Hearts

I have used coloured foil for this heartfelt card. Foil is easily creased while you are working, so use a brayer to smooth it out. You will learn to bend, shape and hammer the wire, punch out metal shapes and use a crimper to corrugate the coloured foil.

This card would make a fabulous wedding anniversary or Valentine card. Or you could simply send it to the one you love.

You will need

Copper metal (1 sheet)

Card: A4 lilac

Purple foil (1 roll)

Copper wire, 18g

Purple wire, 18g

Copper mesh (1 sheet)

Heart punch

Crimper

Hammer and anvil

Round-nosed pliers

Wire cutters

Scissors

Single hole punch

Pencil • Ruler • Plastic eraser

Heating tool • Chopping board

Craft knife

Wide double-sided tape

3D foam tape

Glue pen

All-purpose craft glue

Paper trimmer

Tip
Use wide double-sided tape when sticking the foil to your cards so that you cannot see the edges of the tape through the foil.

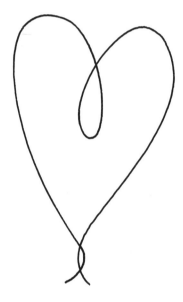

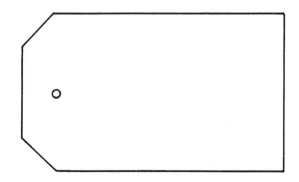

The patterns for the wire heart, luggage label and tag

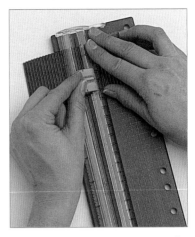

1. Use a paper trimmer to cut two rectangles of purple foil 8 x 5.5cm, (3¼ x 2¼in). Then cut a third rectangle 12.5 x 5.5cm (5in x 2¼in). This extra length allows for crimping.

2. Crimp the long rectangle using the crimper.

3. Cut the crimped rectangle to the same size as the other two rectangles, using a paper trimmer.

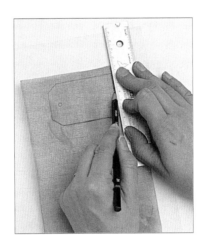

4. Trace the label shape on to copper mesh. Cut out the shape using scissors.

5. Heat the mesh label using the heating tool. Make sure you hold the mesh down with a tool, such as a craft knife, or the heat will blow it around. Note that mesh changes colour much more quickly than metal, so heat it with care.

6. Heat a piece of copper. Punch three heart shapes out of the copper, using a special punch.

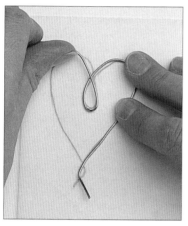

7. Bend and shape the copper wire into a large heart, using the pattern as a guide.

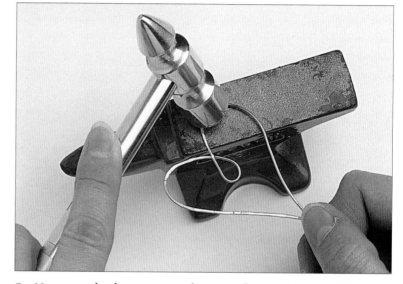

8. Hammer the large copper heart to flatten the wire. The hammer will leave marks on the wire, so you will need to turn the heart over when you mount it on the card.

9. Cut a length of purple 18g wire using wire cutters. Bend and shape it for the luggage label tag using round-nosed pliers. Then hammer the wire in the same way as you did the wire heart.

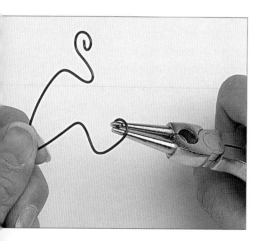

10. Stick all three pieces of purple foil to the card using wide double-sided tape.

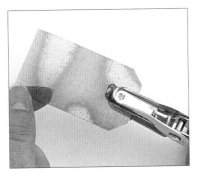

11. Punch a hole in the mesh luggage label using a single hole punch.

12. Punch three heart shapes out of purple foil. Stick the hearts to the luggage label using bits of 3D foam tape. Feed the luggage label wire accent through the hole.

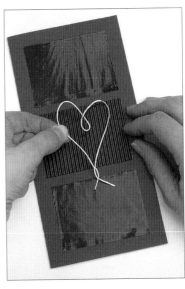

13. Glue the hammered wire heart down, using all-purpose craft glue, and leave to dry.

14. Apply small strips of double-sided tape to the reverse of the luggage label, behind the hearts, and stick the luggage label on to the foil rectangle at the top of the card. If double-sided tape is used to secure mesh, it should always be used behind an accent in this way, or it will show through the mesh.

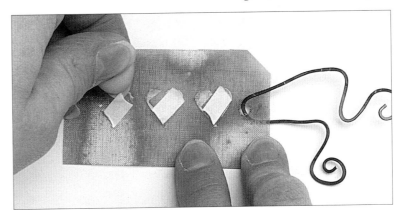

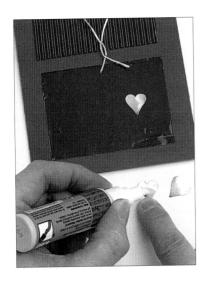

15. Use a glue pen to apply glue to the reverse of the copper hearts, and stick them in place on the bottom foil panel as shown.

The finished heart card.
Opposite
This card, envelope and luggage label use shaped and hammered wire in the same way as the project, but mix hearts and spirals to create a different look.

Golden Fossil

Whilst on holiday in Lyme Regis, Dorset with my family and close friend, Melanie, we did what everyone does in Lyme Regis – we hammered for fossils. We were lucky enough to find several, and the result is this card.

I used gold embossing foil, as it is thinner than the metal sheets and takes the rubbed impression really well. I also collected sea shells with my son, Owen, in Devon, and used them in the same way on some other cards, shown on pages 44–45.

Tip
Rubbings from tree bark, special buttons and carved images all make ideal three-dimensional features for use with foil.

The pattern for the luggage label

You will need
Copper metal (1 sheet)
18g turquoise wire
Gold embossing foil
C6 size copper-coloured card
Chocolate bar foil wrapper
Skeleton leaf
Fossil
Scissors
Deckle-edged scissors
Pencil
Plastic eraser
Tracing paper
Embossing tool
Wooden tool
Foam sheet
Heating tool
Chopping board
Metal ruler
Double-sided tape
Spray mount
3D fluid
Craft knife
Single hole punch

1. Take a piece of gold embossing foil and cut out a square slightly larger than your fossil.

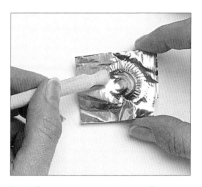

2. Place your square of embossing foil over your fossil and use a wooden tool to rub over the surface to create an impression.

3. Pick out the finer details of the fossil using the larger end of an embossing tool.

4. Hammer the edges of the fossil foil using the medium point of your embossing tool.

5. Using fancy-edged scissors, cut a deckle edge around the embossed square, and then cut v-shapes into the edges to give the appearance of torn, aged paper.

6. Turn the embossed foil over and fill the indentation with 3D fluid. Leave it to dry, preferably overnight but for at least two to three hours, depending on how deep the embossing is.

Tip
3D fluid is cloudy when wet, but becomes clear as it dries.

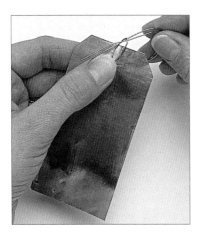  

7. Trace, cut out and heat a copper luggage label shape, and use a single hole punch to punch the hole. Take a piece of wire and double it. Feed the loop through the luggage label hole and feed the two free ends through the loop.

8. Tear a piece of gold chocolate wrapper slightly larger than the luggage label. Scrunch it up to give it a crumpled look and then lay it flat.

9. Spray the reverse of the foil wrapper with spray mount and stick it to the card.

10. Apply double-sided tape and stick the luggage label to the foil. Stick the skeleton leaf to the luggage label using a small piece of double-sided tape in the place that will be concealed by the fossil foil. Then put two strips of double-sided tape on the back of the fossil foil and stick it on top of the leaf.

This project always reminds me of the wonderful day we had in Lyme Regis, where we found the ammonite fossil. The blue of the skeleton leaf sets off the burnished colour of the heated copper, and the gold, combined with the copper background, gives a wonderful rich feel to the card.

The cards I make using found objects always make me smile, as they remind me of the fun I had finding them. The shell cards are the result of a glorious sunny day on the beach at Dawlish, Devon, paddling with my son, Owen and collecting shells. The card on the far right shows a rubbing of an elephant taken from a wooden block stamp I found in an amazing shop at an arts centre in Tubac, Arizona. Enjoy creating cards with your own found objects, and they will bring back happy memories for you, too.

Further techniques

There are many other techniques which combine metal and wire. Here are a few to inspire your own creativity.

Piercing Use a fine piercing tool to make holes in the metal and coloured foils and create different patterns.

Add **3D paint** to your cards. This will stay raised and dimensional when dry, giving both depth and highlights to your work.

Rubber stamping combines beautifully with the metals and coloured foils. Stamp on the metals or foils using permanent inks and emboss around the outline of the stamped image. Rubber stamping can also be used to create backgrounds for your metal and wire cards.

Enjoy working with metal and wire, taking the techniques to new levels, but above all, have fun!

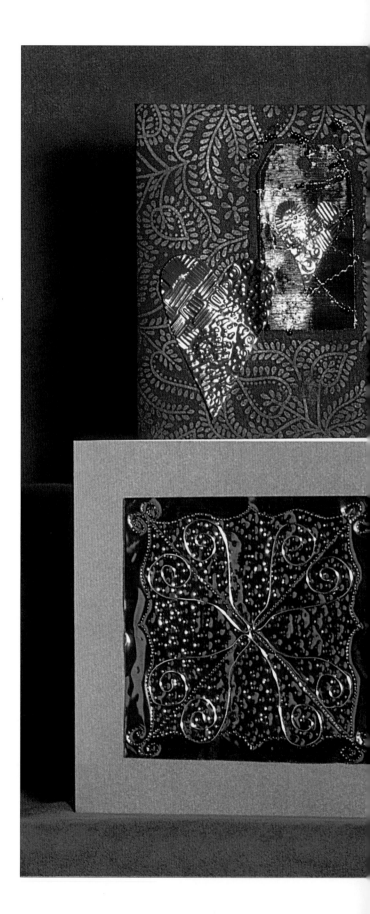

Index